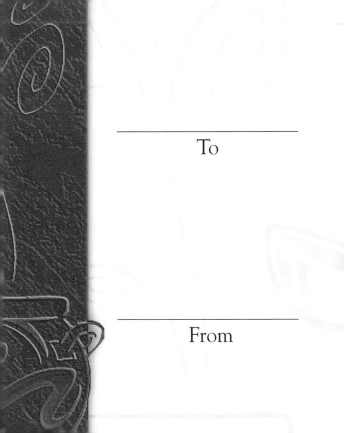

To

From

A LITTLE SPOONFUL OF CHICKEN SOUP FOR THE SOUL®

Copyright © 1998 Chicken Soup For The Soul Enterprises, Inc.

All Rights Reserved.

Published by Blessings Unlimited, Pentagon Towers
P.O. Box 398004, Edina, MN 55439

Design by Kim Hokanson

ISBN 1-58375-433-4
Printed in Mexico

A Little Spoonful of

Chicken Soup
for the Soul

One at a Time

A friend of ours was walking down a deserted Mexican beach at sunset. As he walked along, he began to see another man in the distance. As he drew nearer, he noticed that the local native kept leaning down, picking something up and throwing it out into the water. Time and again he kept hurling things out into the ocean.

As our friend approached even closer, he noticed that the man was picking up starfish that had been washed up on the beach and, one at a time, he was throwing them back into the water.

Our friend was puzzled. He approached the man and said, "Good evening, friend. I was wondering what you are doing."

"I'm throwing these starfish back into the ocean. You see, it's low tide right now and all of these starfish have been washed up onto the shore. If I don't throw them back into the sea, they'll die up here from lack of oxygen."

"I understand," my friend replied, "but there must be thousands of starfish on this beach. You can't possibly get to all of them. There are simply too many. And don't you realize this is probably happening on hundreds of beaches all up and down this coast. Can't you see that you can't possibly make a difference?"

The local native smiled, bent down and picked up yet another starfish, and as he threw it back into the sea, he replied, "Made a difference to that one!"

—*Jack Canfield and Mark V. Hansen*
Chicken Soup for the Soul

**The Meaning of things
lies not in the things themselves,
but in our attitude towards them.**

Antoine de Saint-Exupéry

A Brother Like That

A friend of mine named Paul
received an automobile from his
brother as a Christmas present.
On Christmas Eve when Paul came
out of his office, a [young boy] was
walking around the shiny new car,
admiring it. "Is this your car, Mister?"
he asked.

Paul nodded. "My brother
gave it to me for Christmas." The
boy was astounded. "You mean

your brother gave it to you and it didn't cost you nothing? Boy, I wish..." He hesitated.

Of course Paul knew what he was going to wish for. He was going to wish he had a brother like that. But what the lad said jarred Paul all the way down to his heels.

"I wish," the boy went on, "that I could be a brother like that."

Paul looked at the boy in astonishment, then impulsively

he added, "Would you like to take a ride in my automobile?"

"Oh yes, I'd love that."

After a short ride, the boy turned and with his eyes aglow said, "Mister, would you mind driving in front of my house?"

Paul smiled a little. He thought he knew what the lad wanted. He wanted to show his neighbors that he could ride home in a big automobile. But Paul was wrong again.

"Will you stop where those two steps are?" the boy asked.

He ran up the steps. Then in a little while Paul heard him coming back, but he was not coming fast. He was carrying his little crippled brother. He sat him down on the bottom step, then sort of squeezed up against him and pointed to the car.

"There she is, Buddy, just

like I told you upstairs. His brother
gave it to him for Christmas and it
didn't cost him a cent. And some
day I'm gonna give you one just like
it...then you can see for yourself all
the pretty things in the Christmas
windows that I've been trying to
tell you about."

Paul got out and lifted
the lad to the front seat of his car.
The shining-eyed older brother
climbed in beside him and the

three of them began a memorable
holiday ride.

That Christmas Eve, Paul
learned what Jesus meant when
he had said: "It is more blessed
to give...."

— *Dan Clark*
Chicken Soup for the Soul

It is the heart that makes a man rich.

He is rich according to what he is,

not according to what he has.

Henry Ward Beecher

A Simple
Gesture

*Everybody can be great...because
anybody can serve. You don't have to have
a college degree to serve. You don't have to
make your subject and verb agree to serve.
You only need a heart full of grace.
A soul generated by love.*

DR. MARTIN LUTHER KING, JR.

Mark was walking home from
school one day when he noticed the

boy ahead of him had tripped and dropped all of the books he was carrying, along with two sweaters, a baseball bat, a glove, and a small tape recorder. Mark knelt down and helped the boy pick up the scattered articles. Since they were going the same way, he helped to carry part of the burden. As they walked, Mark discovered the boy's name was Bill, that he loved video games, baseball and history, that he was having a lot of trouble with his other subjects and that he had just broken up with his girlfriend.

They arrived at Bill's home first and Mark was invited in for a Coke and to watch some television. The afternoon passed pleasantly with a few laughs and some shared small talk, then Mark went home.

They continued to see each other around school, had lunch together once or twice, then both graduated from junior high school. They ended up in the same high school where they had brief contacts over the years. Finally the long awaited senior year came, and three weeks before graduation, Bill asked Mark if they could talk.

Bill reminded him of the day

years ago when they had first met.
"Do you ever wonder why I was
carrying so many things home that
day?" asked Bill. "You see, I cleaned
out my locker because I didn't want
to leave a mess for anyone else. I
had stored away some of my mother's
sleeping pills and I was going home
to commit suicide. But after we
spent some time together talking
and laughing, I realized that if I had

killed myself, I would have missed that time and so many others that might follow. So you see, Mark, when you picked up my books that day, you did a lot more. You saved my life."

— *John W. Schlatter*
Chicken Soup for the Soul

A thousand words will
not leave so deep an
impression as one deed.

Henrik Ibsen

Puppies
for Sale

A store owner was tacking
a sign above his door that read
"Puppies For Sale." Signs like
that have a way of attracting small
children, and sure enough, a little
boy appeared under the store
owner's sign. "How much are you
going to sell the puppies for?"
he asked.

The store owner replied,
"Anywhere from $30 to $50."

The little boy reached in his

pocket and pulled out some change. "I have $2.37," he said. "Can I please look at them?"

The store owner smiled and whistled and out of the kennel came Lady, who ran down the aisle of his store followed by five teeny, tiny balls of fur. One puppy was lagging considerably behind. Immediately the little boy singled out the lagging, limping puppy and said, "What's wrong with that little dog?"

The store owner explained that the veterinarian had examined the little puppy and had discovered it didn't have a hip socket. It would always be lame. The little boy became excited. "That is the puppy that I want to buy."

The store owner said, "No, you don't want to buy that little dog. If you really want him, I'll just give him to you."

The little boy got quite upset.

He looked straight into the store owner's eyes, pointed his finger and said, "I don't want you to give him to me. That little dog is worth every bit as much as all the other dogs and I'll pay full price. In fact, I'll give you $2.37 now, and 50 cents a month until I have him paid for."

The store owner countered, "You really don't want to buy this little dog. He is never going to be able to run and jump and play with you like the other puppies."

To this, the little boy reached down and rolled up his pant leg to reveal a badly twisted, crippled left leg supported by a big metal brace. He looked up at the store owner and softly replied, "Well, I don't run so well myself, and the little puppy will need someone who understands!"

— *Dan Clark, Weathering the Storm*
Chicken Soup for the Soul

Nouns
and
Adverbs

Hope is the parent of faith!

CYRUS AUGUSTUS BARTOL

Several years ago, a public school teacher was hired and assigned to visit children who were patients in a large city hospital. Her job was to tutor them with their school work so they wouldn't be too far behind when well enough to return to school.

One day, this teacher received
a routine call requesting that she visit
a particular child. She took the boy's
name, hospital and room number
and was told by the teacher on the
other end of the line, "We're studying
nouns and adverbs in class now. I'd
be grateful if you could help him
with his homework so he doesn't
fall behind the others."

It wasn't until the visiting
teacher got outside the boy's room

that she realized it was located in the hospital's burn unit. No one had prepared her for what she was about to discover on the other side of the door. Before she was allowed to enter, she had put on a sterile hospital gown and cap because of the possibility of infection. She was told not to touch the boy or his bed. She could stand near but must speak through the mask she had to wear.

    When she had finally

completed all the preliminary washings and was dressed in the prescribed coverings, she took a deep breath and walked into the room. The young boy, horribly burned, was obviously in great pain. The teacher felt awkward and didn't know what to say, but she had gone too far to turn around and walk out. Finally she was able to stammer out, "I'm the special visiting hospital teacher, and your teacher sent me to help you with your nouns and adverbs." Afterward, she thought it was not one of her more successful tutoring sessions.

The next morning when she returned, one of the nurses on the burn unit asked her, "What did you do to that boy?"

Before she could finish a profusion of apologies, the nurse interrupted her by saying, "You don't understand. We've been worried about him, but ever since you were here yesterday his whole attitude has changed. He's fighting back, responding to treatment...it's as though he's decided to live."

The boy himself later explained that he had completely given up hope and felt he was going to die, until he saw that special teacher. Everything had changed with an insight gained by a simple realization. With happy tears in his eyes, the little boy who had been burned so badly that he had given up hope, expressed it like this: "They wouldn't send a special teacher to work on nouns and adverbs with a dying boy, now, would they?"

— Excerpted from Moments with Mothers
A 4th Course of Chicken Soup for the Soul

Blessed Are the Pure in Heart

Blessed are the pure in heart.
So often we are told
Of saints whose names and daily deeds
Inscribed in books of gold
Are certain to be seeing God
In well-rewarding joy—
But when I see the pure in heart
I see a little boy.

He shins up trees and barks his knees,
Has lizards in a box;

He loves to read of dinosaurs,
Collects bright-colored rocks.
His grubby hands are gentle
On the coats of dogs and birds,
And he has a quiet wisdom
in naiveté of words.
I listen to his little prayers
At night with quiet joy—
And when I hear the pure in heart
I hear a little boy.

He hasn't reached the age as yet
To question and to doubt;
He gravely takes his mother's words,
And that's what life's about.
Each day is gold, a shining thing
Without a wrong alloy—
And when I hold the pure in heart
I hold a little boy.

— *Gwen Belson Taylor*
A 5th Course of Chicken Soup for the Soul

Night
Watch

"Your son is here," the nurse said to the old man. She had to repeat the words several times before the man's eyes opened. He was heavily sedated and only partially conscious after a massive heart attack he had suffered the night before. He could see the dim outline of a young man in a Marine Corps uniform, standing alongside his bed.

The old man reached out his hand. The Marine wrapped his toughened fingers around the old man's limp hand and squeezed gently. The nurse brought a chair, and the tired serviceman sat down at the bedside.

All through the night, the young Marine sat in the poorly

lighted ward, holding the old man's hand and offering words of encouragement. The dying man said nothing, but kept a feeble grip on the young man's hand. Oblivious to the noise of the oxygen tank, the moans of the other patients, and the bustle of the night staff coming in and out of the ward, the Marine remained at the old man's side.

Every now and then, when she stopped by to check on her patients, the nurse heard the young Marine whisper a few comforting words to the old man. Several times in the course of that long night, she returned and suggested that the Marine leave to rest for a while. But every time, the young man refused.

Near dawn the old man died. The Marine placed the old man's lifeless hand on the bed and left to find the nurse. While the nurse took the old man away and attended to the necessary duties, the young man waited. When the nurse returned, she began to offer words of sympathy, but the Marine interrupted her.

"Who was that man?" he asked.

Startled, the nurse replied, "He was your father."

"No, he wasn't," the young man said. "I've never seen him before in my life."

"Then why didn't you say

something when I took you to see him?"

"I knew there had been a mistake by the people who sent me home on an emergency furlough. What happened was, there were two of us with the same name, from the same town and we had similar serial numbers. They sent me by mistake," the young man explained. "But I also knew he needed his son, and his son wasn't there. I could tell he was too sick to know whether I was his son or not. When I realized how much he needed to have someone there, I just decided to stay."

— *Roy Popkin*
A 5th Course of Chicken Soup for the Soul

An
Afternoon
in the
Park

There once was a little boy who wanted to meet God. He knew it was a long trip to where God lived, so he packed his suitcase with Twinkies and a six-pack of root beer and he started his journey.

When he had gone about three blocks, he met an old woman. She was sitting in the park just staring at some pigeons. The boy sat down next to her and opened his suitcase. He was about to take a drink from his root beer when he noticed that the old lady looked hungry, so he offered her a Twinkie. She gratefully accepted it and smiled at him. Her smile was so pretty that the boy wanted to see it again, so he offered her a root beer. Once again she smiled at him. The boy was delighted!

They sat there all afternoon eating and smiling, but they never said a word.

As it grew dark, the boy

realized how tired he was and he got up to leave, but before he had gone more than a few steps, he turned around, ran back to the old woman and gave her a hug. She gave him her biggest smile ever.

When the boy opened the door to his own house a short time later, his mother was surprised by the look of joy on his face.

She asked him, "What did you do today that made you so

happy?"

He replied, "I had lunch with God." But before his mother could respond, he added, "You know what? She's got the most beautiful smile I've ever seen!"

Meanwhile, the old woman, also radiant with joy, returned to her home.

Her son was stunned by the look of peace on her face and he asked, "Mother, what did you do today that made you so happy?"

She replied, "I ate Twinkies in the park with God." But before her son responded, she added, "You know, he's much younger than I expected."

— Julie A. Manhan
A 3rd Course of Chicken Soup for the Soul

The
Prettiest
Angel

For the past 20 years I have spoken to all kinds of audiences in the character of Benjamin Franklin. Even though the majority of my engagements are before corporate and convention audiences, I still like to talk to school groups. When I work for corporate clients outside the Philadelphia area, I ask them to sponsor appearances in two schools as a service to their community.

I find that even very young children relate well to the message I present through the character of Benjamin Franklin. I always encourage them to ask any questions they wish, so I usually get some interesting ones. The character of Benjamin Franklin often becomes so real to these students that they willingly suspend disbelief and are caught up in a dialogue with me as if I am really Ben Franklin.

On one particular day after an assembly for an elementary school, I was visiting a fifth-grade classroom to answer questions for students who were studying American history. One student raised his hand and said, "I thought you died." This was not an unusual question and I answered it by saying, "Well, I did die on April 17, 1790, when I was 84 years old, but I didn't like it and I'm never going to do it again."

I immediately asked for any other questions and called on a boy at the back of the room who raised his hand. He asked, "When you were in Heaven, did you see my mother there?"

My heart stopped. I wanted the floor to open up and swallow me. My only thought was, "Don't blow this!" I realized for an 11-year-old boy to ask that question in front of all of his classmates it had to either be a very recent occurrence or of utmost concern. I also knew I had to say something.

Then I heard my voice say: "I'm not sure if she is the one I think she was, but if she is, she was the prettiest angel there."

The smile on his face told me that it was the right answer. I'm not

sure where it came from, but I think
I just may have had a little help from
the prettiest angel there.

— *Ralph Archbold*
A 2nd Helping of Chicken Soup for the Soul